You Are Favor

You Are Favor

Andrea Renee'

TUCKER
PUBLISHING HOUSE LLC

Copyright page

ISBN: 978-1-7344526-2-4

Book Credits:

Cover Photography: James Witcher

Cover Model: Janaya Claxton

Graphic Designer: Richard Dodds

Model Make-Up Artist: Marv Dixon

Model Hair: Kiara James

Model Stylist: Andrea Renee'

Author Photographer: Alexis Cole

Author Stylist: Andrea Renee'

Author Make-Up Artist: Moriah Mierre

Author Book Coach: Tara Tucker

Publishing Company: Tucker Publishing House, LLC

www.tuckerpublishinghouse.com

Table of Contents

Dedication

I would like to dedicate "You Are Favor" to both of my grandmothers, Olivia, and Nona. They meant the world to me, and they still do even though they are no longer on the earth. The quality time I was privileged to experience with each of them is something I will never forget. The conversations we had, and their infectious laughs are etched in my memory forever.

I am so grateful that I had the two best grandmothers in the entire world. They made sure they let me know how much they loved me, and I tried my best to show them how much I loved and appreciated them! I honor their memory. The love they both had for me still motivates and inspires me to accomplish my goals. I miss my two loves. I move forward in the faith and love that they taught me.

Introduction

I have always heard the saying that if you have not found the book that you're looking to read, it is most likely meant for you to write it. *You Are Favor* was birthed out of pain. I have always had the desire to encourage and uplift others. It's just a part of me. Anyone who has a desire to help others usually experiences circumstances that cause discouragement. I have had a ton of discouraging experiences in my lifetime that have left me wondering why I had to go through such heartache. Although I have experienced difficulties, that does not make me damaged goods.

I have learned that pain molds us, shapes us, and grows us if we allow it to. In this book, you will find the strength needed to make it through embarrassing situations, and circumstances that just seem unfair.

It doesn't matter where you find yourself in life,

God's favor is present.

> *You have to believe it. You have to*
> *know it. You have to walk in it.*

You are enough!

Life does not end at the sight of difficulty, it's at that point that it begins.

Enjoy!

Andrea Renee'

A Beautiful Resuscitation

God is the breath of life. Without Him providing breath for our lungs, we would cease to be. Although we need breath to be alive physically, I would like to discuss the breath that God can breathe into us when we feel completely dead inside. A living, walking, zombie. Alive, but there is no life because of disappointment and heartbreak.

A friend of mine relayed a message to me of what her sister-in-law said she saw concerning my future. The phrase was "a beautiful resuscitation."

At this time, I am certainly being brought back to life. I have spent a lot of my time helping others build. That statement is not a complaint, it is an observation. I love that God placed a longing to help and assist inside of me, because when you make yourself available in building up others, the reward is truly priceless.

Today, I am allowing God to breathe new life into parts of me that I thought were dead. I see myself writing, singing, speaking, and traveling the world again. I can envision me living out the original intent and purpose God had in mind when He created me. Honestly, I'd lost that part of myself. The fiery, driven part of me that was going after everything God purposed for me no matter what.

Although I am full of hope and joy about the future in this current moment; everything about my bank account and my circumstances says this "new life" is impossible! But, through the eyes of faith, impossible things are truly possible.

> *For with God nothing will be impossible. Luke 1:37 NKJV*

- What are you experiencing right now that seems impossible to be resolved?
- What dream(s) have you allowed to die?

- What are your dreams? Jot them down.
- Who has decided to walk out of your life, and it has taken your breath away?
- What areas of your existence need the breath of life?

Breathe Again

This is one thing that I have learned and something that I stand on, even in challenging times; there is absolutely nothing too hard for God. When you really take a moment and allow that truth to resonate within you, God's peace is then able to sit down right beside you and wrap His arms around you.

With a resuscitation, there must be contact. The person needing help is usually unconscious and unaware that they need assistance. The individual is unable to signal for help or scream out in agony, because they are literally having trouble breathing. To resuscitate, the person without air needs someone to rescue them and breathe into them. Once it's realized that the person needs resuscitation, the person helping usually requests space or room to work. He/she will ask everyone to back up, to properly assist, and not encounter any distractions that could result in death.

When you lose someone dear to you, experience depression, your marriage fails, or even when you lose everything you have worked so hard for; these are instances when you can feel the zeal you once had for life slowly leaving you. God then asks everyone and everything that could cause distractions to back up, so that He can breathe into you, privately. He breathes new life into your spirit by His Word. That personal time with Him allows Him to heal, renew, restore, and regenerate you. As He begins to breathe words of life and you begin to believe what He has said, you become a conscious participant, instead of an unconscious one.

When I was battling depression, God sent

people that were able to speak life into me at the right time. It would usually be right at that moment when I felt so alone and so hopeless, that God would send someone to "see me." The person would be able to see right where I was, and they took the time to resuscitate me, whether it was with their words, prayers, or simply taking the time to listen. It was always perfect timing. It was needed. It revived me.

The world is currently facing a Pandemic. I am sitting in my bedroom by a window, writing. Most of my days are spent in solitude, besides the times I am on the phone or on social media. Like many of us, I am not working, so time is something that I have a lot of. There are no major present distractions in my life. I am separated from my husband, and this position in life is not something that I wanted or even desired, but it is my reality. I certainly would love to be with my husband weathering the storms of life together, but that is not the case currently.

Although I would love to be working, and have a steady income flowing, it is all quite different in my life right now. Although, the times are difficult and uncertain; God has allowed me to have some very intimate moments with Him. God has certainly revealed Himself as Jehovah Jireh in my life.

Did I mention churches are "closed" too? Although we don't get to choose how God orchestrates certain things in our lives, I

believe His hand is in it all. I never thought the time that I wanted to have with God alone would come this way, ever. I am thankful that He is renewing, restoring, and regenerating me. I am no longer unconscious; I am an active participant in my strengthening process. I believe what He has said concerning my life and my future.

Once the Word really penetrates your heart and you begin the process of renewing your mind; that is when the beauty of new life begins.

Don't copy the behavior and

*customs of this world, but let
God transform you into a new
person by changing the way you
think. Then you will learn to
know God's will for you, which is
good and pleasing and perfect.*
Romans 12:2 NLT

There is a beautiful exchange that can occur between you and God once you open your heart to Him. He promised in His Word to give beauty in exchange for our ashes.

*And provide for those who grieve
in Zion---- to bestow on them a
crown of beauty instead of
ashes, the oil of joy instead of
mourning, and a garment of
praise instead of despair....*
Isaiah 61:3 NIV

Authentic Beauty

God desires to give us beauty in exchange for things that have disintegrated in our lives, right before our eyes.

Relationships hold deep importance in our lives, they are essential to our growth and quality of life. We are not meant to be alone. When relationships end or appear to be at the end; that reality is gut-wrenching. Especially if you have invested time and love into it.

I have heard many people describe the divorce process as being equivalent to death. But, even in that space of not knowing whether the relationship will survive or end; there is hope and peace available. A separation can be ugly in the sense that your emotions and thoughts are all over the place. You will feel embarrassed, you will feel alone, you will feel ashamed, and you will not want many to know what is occurring in your life. I know what this feels like because I am experiencing it right now. Yet, God has given me strength. He has encouraged me to do the work needed to become whole.

I am a huge advocate for marriage, and I always have been, and I will continue to be. I believe in "till death do us part." I saw both sets of my grandparents live out their vows, so I know it

can be done. It can be accomplished through love, understanding, and the release of pride and true humility. I love the beautiful example that I had in them. So, imagine my dismay as I sit here writing this book and my marriage is on the brinks of ending.

Remember, I said earlier that I have learned that God can do absolutely anything? Nothing is too hard for Him! There are times we stand in faith and believe that things will work in the favor we are praying for and there will be a positive outcome. But what if the marriage does not survive? What will be your stance then? What will be your declaration? Even if things come to an end, God still could have worked the miracle. A marriage failing is not a reflection that God's power does not work, or that He is not capable. Some things in our lives just don't go as planned. Tragedies occur, marriages end, and people transition from this life to eternity.

But I absolutely love the Word because even if the outcome is unfavorable, God promises that it will all work together for good.

> *And we know that all things work together for good to those who love God, to those who are the called according to His purpose. Romans 8:28 NKJV*

Do you know what that means? That means even if your breath is taken away for a moment because of disappointment; God has promised that He will cause it to be "good." I know, that sounds absolutely crazy! How in the world can death, divorce, or depression be good? The situations by themselves are not good, they are tragic and heartbreaking. But, when you add a wonderful, excellent, loving Savior to the equation, who has your best interest in His heart; it's simply good.

He takes each detail of our lives (good and bad) and weaves them together to make even the most horrific situations good because of the commitment of love. There is so much benefit to serving God, His Kingdom, and loving Him with all your heart, soul, and mind.

> *Jesus replied: Love the Lord your*
> *God with all your heart and with all*
> *your soul and with all your mind.*
> Matthew 22:37 NIV

Simply because you love God and you're striving to live according to His purpose, He promises that beauty will emerge from tragedy. Resuscitation requires someone stronger than you to breathe into you. God gently takes our tired soul and reassures us that the situations we face will not kill us but strengthen us.

Our Savior is strong enough to handle even our most heart-breaking experiences. There is not one thing that you will go through that has caught Him by surprise or has caught Him off-guard. He knows it all. He sees it all. You can trust Him to breathe life back into you. He won't laugh at your mistakes or mock you when you fall. He will lovingly take you into His arms and gently breathe life back into you. Ask Him to help you, He is right there.

The Lord is near to the
brokenhearted and saves the crushed
in spirit. Psalm 34:18 ESV

Prayer: God, thank you for the one reading this prayer. Thank You that You are doing a marvelous work in them right now. Thank You that Your presence is comforting them. When we have to deal with the ugliness of life, it can be overwhelming, and it has the capacity to take our breath away. Sometimes, we have to wrestle with things that are hard, things we don't understand. You promised that You would help us through situations that look and feel impossible. You are a very present help in the time of trouble (Psalm 46:1). You are our refuge and our strength. Help us to realize that walking with You is not always glamorous, sometimes it's hard and sometimes we will feel like giving up. But God, You are our hope! Help us to realize that with You nothing is impossible, Your Word says that it is indeed possible. We need the beautiful exchange You promised in Your Word. God, we give You our ashes, please give us beauty! Beauty that can't be denied. Beauty that is visible from the inside out! Shine Your light of truth in us! Let our lives and our walk with You bring You glory, in Jesus name, amen.

Your Legacy

When most of us think of legacy, we think of children, grandchildren, great-grandchildren, and the generations to come. We think of how beautiful it is to witness generation after generation being born into the world. We want to see our sons and daughters grow their families by being fruitful and multiplying.

On the other hand, there are those of us who desire to begin a family, but it has not happened yet. We are waiting. We don't know what our "wait" will look like, but we trust the God who knows the end from the beginning.

God often uses pain and waiting to build us up, restore, and renew us. I know! It sounds backwards. Why would God use the pain and the agony of waiting on something we want to mature us? He uses it because He loves us, and

He wants us to deeply discover His strength and not lean to our own.

> *Trust in the LORD with all your heart and lean not on your own understanding. Proverbs 3:5 NIV*

God is inviting us in on receiving the greatest strength of all, *His*. Think about it. Without the cross, without the sacrifice that Jesus made to die for us; we would be lost. Jesus had to go through pain, for the promise of salvation and eternal life to be given to us. Out of His pain and agony, something beautiful and eternal was birthed. There was a specific hour chosen by God for His Son Jesus to die. So, Jesus had to wait for that appointed time. He could not rush it, hurry it along, or pray for it to come faster. There was a time set in eternity, and Jesus had to wait until that time was fulfilled on the earth.

Trust seems like it should be simple with God, but because we are human; it becomes complicated. Why wouldn't I trust the God Who made heaven and the earth? Why wouldn't I completely and totally lean on Him instead of my own thoughts and understanding of circumstances?

Often, I have heard people say that trust must be earned; it is not automatically given. Well, with trusting God, that portion of our heart should certainly be automatically given and submitted to Him. Why? God has already proven that He is indeed trustworthy, repeatedly. God keeps His Word, He cannot lie. The bible says that heaven and earth will pass away, but by no means will His Word pass away. (*Matthew 24:35*)

God does not lie, and He does not contain the ability to lie.

> *God is not man, that He should lie; neither the son of man, that He should repent: hath He said, and shall He not do it? Or hath He spoken, and shall He not make it good? Numbers 23:19*

KJV

At this moment, I have no idea whether I will ever carry (to full-term) and deliver biological children. As I mentioned before, I am not physically with my husband. I am not with the one that I thought that I would begin a family with. I don't know the outcome of this portion of my life, but I trust God. He is trustworthy. You can trust what He says, you can trust how He moves in your life, you can trust His plan for you!

On June 12th, 2018, I experienced a miscarriage. It was my first pregnancy, my first time being able to say that I was pregnant. For a long time, it was difficult for me to even utter

the word, "miscarriage." My heart would drop and the pain the word carried would be felt throughout my entire body.

Prior to becoming pregnant, I suffered from a condition called Vaginismus. The basis of the condition is that you are unable to have sexual intercourse due to anxiety. Penetration is impossible. In March of 2018 in New York, I was cured of Vaginismus; after suffering through the condition for almost ten years of marriage. Being cured was a major victory in my life. It was the elephant that followed me wherever I went and sat with me unknowingly, most of my life until it was finally dismissed.

June 5th, 2018 turned out to be the day that I found I was pregnant. During the early parts of May 2018, I noticed that I was throwing up randomly, feeling completely turned off at the sight of certain foods, having awful headaches, feeling lightheaded at times, and craving watermelon. I cannot stand watermelon, so I

new something was going on. I decided to wait until I was late for my cycle for at least seven days so that I could get a more accurate home pregnancy test result. Once I was ready to take the test, I took about five of them because I wanted to be sure! Turns out, I was indeed pregnant. Double lines everywhere! The next day, I called my doctor's office and made an appointment for the first ultrasound.

The very next week on June 12th, 2018 around three o'clock in the morning, I woke up bleeding. My heart stopped at that moment. I was startled and scared. I was devastated because I knew I was having a miscarriage.

I got up out of the bed and the blood was running down my legs. I could not believe that this was happening to me. I was losing the baby, the child, the future that I wanted so bad.

After coming out of the bathroom, I laid back down in the bed. I was staring at the ceiling, with hot tears running down my cheeks and silent prayers being said in my heart until eight o' clock in the morning. I knew the doctor's office was open and I knew my manager would answer my text message stating that I would not be coming into work that day.

The doctor instructed me to come in as soon as possible. I was still bleeding heavily. I knew I was not pregnant anymore. If I could explain what it felt like; it felt like "life" was slowly leaving my body. It felt like hope, excitement and joy had turned their back on me and I was just left with deep sadness and despair.

I arrived at the office, and as I walked in; there staring back at me were women in their second and third trimesters in the waiting room. I was still bleeding. My heart broke some more. I was reminded once again, of what I was unable to carry to full-term.

The grace and love of God is so real. Even in that moment, I asked God to please help me to not become bitter. I was hurting, but I did not want to live a bitter life. I did not want to resent seeing pregnant women and their babies in the future. God is gracious because I know that prayer originated from His love for me. I was broken, but He knew I needed to invite Him into my future so that I did not become someone He never intended for me to be. God helps us walk through our brokenness but overall, our Father wants us whole.

The nurse opened the door widely, yet in slow motion with my medical history folder in hand and called my name to go back. Everything was in movie-style slow motion. The way I got up, the way I looked at my husband, the way each footstep took forever as I walked to the back following the nurse. It was all just really slow and dream-like. I could not believe it. I was in shock.

Once we arrived in the back, the nurse drew my blood, but I already knew the results. The amount of blood I had lost, was too much for a fetus to survive. The flow was heavy. After she was done drawing my blood, she said, "We will call you with the results." I wanted to respond and tell her that there was no need for the heart-breaking call, I already knew. Instead, I just nodded in agreement and walked out.

The hospital where I would have delivered the baby was remarkably close to the doctor's office. A part of me wanted to see where I would have delivered the baby. I wanted to see with my own eyes where our child would have entered the world in February of 2019. So, we went. We parked, we walked in and we sat in the main waiting area near labor and delivery for a few moments. To this day if you asked me why I requested that visit, I could not tell you. I just wanted to be there. It was definitely one of those peculiar grief moves. If you have ever experienced deep grief, then you can relate. Your mind and your body may operate out of sync. It's the result of shock.

It felt so good to utter the words, "I'm pregnant." I was so excited and looking forward to sharing the amazing news with loved ones. I had shared the news of my condition and struggle with Vaginismus with my loved ones because I wanted their prayers, love, and support. At the time, I was going to be in NYC for almost three weeks; so, I wanted my loved ones to know where I was and what was going on. With finding out I was pregnant, it was a chance to share the good news that the treatment in NYC was successful, and I had tackled another tremendous hurdle in my life.

To finally be on the other side of pregnancy news was one of my greatest experiences in life! Although, the baby did not survive, I do believe that I will be able to declare those words again.

Please know that I asked God numerous times, "Why?!" *Why our first baby? Why now? Why did You allow the pregnancy if it was going to fail? God, after everything we endured to get to this point, why would You allow this to happen to us?* I asked while sobbing, being angry, frustrated and confused. I went from finally experiencing great joy, to once again experiencing great pain. There's that word again, pain.

Although I was going through all the emotions and sorrow connected to a miscarriage, God's Word kept ringing in my heart. His peace wrapped around me so sweetly that all I could do was be thankful and grateful. You may ask, for what? I was thankful for the opportunity to carry a life, even though it wasn't full-term; and I would have to bear the reality that I will never get the chance to see their face. I experienced being pregnant! I had never been able to say that or join in on pregnancy conversations

because it was something that I had never had the privilege of knowing about.

There is no comfort like God's Word. It is calming. It is reassuring. It is full of love and peace. It can and will carry you through even the toughest of life's circumstances.

And the peace of God, which passeth all understanding, shall keep your hearts and minds through Christ Jesus. Philippians 4:7 KJV

I must keep my mind on Him.

People with their minds set on You, You keep completely whole, steady on their feet... Isaiah 26:3 MSG

As I sit here looking out of the window with my laptop comfortably placed in front of me, I have not experienced a second pregnancy yet. I should be hopeless and sad. I should not have the faith that God will still bless me with a biological legacy, but I do. I still believe God can do anything. Without Him, this circumstance does resemble the impossible; but with God all things are possible.

Now, I am not going to hold you up at all. It is a concern of mine that my age is steadily climbing, and I am not actively working on creating a family. Everything around me says my clock is ticking faster and faster. Statistics say that at my age, having a baby is labeled as a "geriatric pregnancy." Geriatric!!! I am still in my 30's! Society, its news and stats will have you in doom and gloom in a hot minute if you let it. I am not letting it.

God calls us to walk by faith and not by sight.

For we walk by faith, not by sight. II Corinthians 5:7 NKJV

I would like to replace the word "walk" with "live" in the scripture. We live by faith, not by sight. When you are living out something, that means that everything that you say and do should reflect/resemble what you are living for. It is a declaration as well as a commitment.

Right now, it does not look like I will ever have children. But my faith must keep my eyes on the fact that God can do anything. Even if I become forty-something, He is still able to do it for me. There will be no time lost in waiting on God. In the wait, I have received strength and have had the opportunity to draw closer to Him. He knows the desire of my heart.

If you are waiting on something and it is painful and confusing. Continue to wait with the right focus. Undoubtedly, there are times that I become discouraged and even weary. I am not saying don't "feel" what you are going through. I am saying feel it all, but don't stay in despair.

Becoming a mother is almost in the same category as getting married and becoming a wife. It is the goal for some. Getting married and having children is a dream most little girls have. To become "wifey" and mommy is something some reach to attain. It is a life goal. Will your worth be diminished if you never become a wife or mother? Absolutely not! If I don't have the privilege of birthing children into this world, I am still worth something. I am still everything that God declares that I am in His Word. I still have value and worth.

What I am learning repeatedly is to not tie my identity and worth to anyone but God! He shapes you; He molds you, He created you, your identity is found in Him!

Can God still be good, and I am not a biological mother? YES.

God's ability, power and favor is not predicated upon what He does for me, it's predicated on Who He is! He is Sovereign! He is Holy! He is love! He is Good, no matter what occurs!

I will have a legacy whether I have children or not because I am living. God allowed me to be on the earth and live. There will be something said about me, the day I take my last breath. There will be words, moments and memories that speak to my lifetime.

Our responsibility is to trust God and His timing. Our lives are already mapped out, we are just discovering the path. Through the pain and the waiting that we all have to endure in life, God is always speaking if we humble ourselves to heed to His voice.

I cannot guarantee that I will birth children, but I believe and trust that God has my best interest in His heart and in His plan for me.

Your worth is not tied to whether or not you birth children into the world. Although, it is honorable just like marriage, you don't become less of a woman if you don't hold these titles. Your worth is found in God alone. What does His Word say about you? Who are you in Him? Once you find out the truth about yourself and believe it, you are limitless! God is causing my foundation to be excavated. Why? Because, only pieces of me believed what His Word says about me.

A friend of mine used the example of home renovation to explain what happens to us when God wants to dig up things in us that should not be there. It is only after the digging that He can plant truth! Truth and lies cannot co-exist. Truth is light and lies survive in darkness. Once a lie is illuminated by the truth, it has to go! Allow God to do the digging. Allow the renovation. Allow Him to rip up and out everything not meant to be in your life. It's the only way to realize and see your God-ordained, predestined legacy come to life.

If you are in a painful place, trust Him and have faith that it will not last forever. If you are in a position of waiting on God to come through, He will. I must warn you that the answer may not come packaged as you expected. Your freedom and deliverance could be presented to you resembling nothing you imagined. It could be hard. It could take years. It could be confusing and heart-breaking, but please know and stand firm on the promise that no matter what it looks like; it is all working together for your good.

Prayer: Father, I come to You asking that You comfort the one reading this. I pray that You would calm her fears and cover her with Your love. Let her know that You are present with her. Reassure her that she is right in the middle of building her legacy even if it does not look like the one, she dreamed of. Please help her to focus on Your goodness! Help her to focus on Your faithfulness! You cannot lie! Heaven and earth will pass away but Your Word stands forever. Give her more joy! Joy for her journey, joy for her testimony and joy for her experiences in You. Yes, we will go through hard times, but with You the hard times are an opportunity to count it all joy.

Consider it pure joy, my sisters, whenever you face trials of many kinds James 1:2 NIV

Help her to seek You for Your strength.

Seek the LORD and His strength.

Seek His face evermore! Psalm 105:4

Prayer: God, a good legacy is something that we all want and desire. Help us to build our legacy on You, a sure foundation, our strong tower. If we build in You, our legacy is guaranteed to stand and be good. Because You are good! Stand with her in the pain and the uncertainty. Comfort her by the power of the Holy Spirit and let her know that You see every tear and every heartbreak. You are concerned about her and You love her.

In Jesus name, amen.

You Are Loved

One of things that we all desire as women is real love. Even if we have been hurt, broken, or disappointed, we still want to be loved. We still want someone to look into our eyes, see us for who we are and express their love for us.

A beautiful truth about God is that He is love. Our Father is literally love.

> *Whoever does not love does not know God, because God is love. I John 4:8 NIV*

There is no possible way that you can be one who does not love others and say that you are a follower of Jesus Christ. There will be times that people will hurt you, and do awful things to you, but you cannot allow that to stop yourself from loving others. Allow the hurt to fuel your love all the more! Take the cross for your example of how to love the unlovable. Jesus loved people that He knew would reject Him and not love Him back. The knowledge of their betrayal did not stop His purpose.

> *But God demonstrates His own*
> *love for us in this: While we were*
> *still sinners, Christ died for us.*
> *Romans 5:8 NIV*

He demonstrated His love for us and died so that we could be free! His love sets us free and it empowers us to love others despite the hurt they may cause us in life. God's love is unconditional. It doesn't change, it doesn't walk away, it doesn't abandon us, and it doesn't condemn us.

If you don't settle yourself in God's love, you will be deceived and believe the lie that no one loves you. There have certainly been times that I have believed the lie. I felt like I was unlovable, I felt invisible, and I felt like no one really saw me for me. If you are not careful and rooted in the Word of God, you can fall prey to these lies meant to steal your joy, kill your confidence, and destroy your future.

In the past, I have researched ways to end my life, and I have attempted suicide. I was in an extremely dark place in my life, and it took God's love to lift me up. I was 23 years old, and I had recently graduated from college about a year prior. I was working at a coffee shop still, and things just felt like they would never improve for me. I believed the lie. I knew God was for me and not against me, but I allowed untruths to enter my heart and mind. Once you open up the door for unbelief, doubt, and discouragement; it can take over.

I was living with a friend, and I had some prescription pain pills that I received from the dentist. I took every single last one of them and sleeping pills.

My friend came home, and she noticed I was extremely lethargic as I was trying to cover up my behavior. She insisted I go to emergency. I reluctantly went because I didn't want anyone to know what I had done, but on the other hand, I didn't want to die. I was scared. I just wanted the pain and disappointment to end.

Once we arrived, they immediately took me back because it was a suicide attempt. I was embarrassed. I was ready to go. I couldn't believe that I had allowed myself to get to this point.

After examination, the decision was made to send me to a facility. The doctor came in and asked me one question, "Do you still feel suicidal?" I said yes. Everything changed after that conversation.

I was placed into an ambulance in the middle of the night. I was by myself. It was just me, God, and my regrets. All I could do was cry. I was in something deep.

When I arrived at the facility and I stood at those double doors, I had no words, just tears. The nurse that checked me in made me give up all my possessions. It was humiliating. I spent forty-eight hours there. The state I lived in typically requests you stay at least seventy-two hours. So, even in me leaving "early," God's hand and grace were still evident in my life. I had no cell phone, all phone calls had to be made on a public phone. Visiting hours were one hour. The food was disgusting. My "roommate" was a dementia patient. I did not sleep one wink while I was there. She would get up all times of the night and wander. I was afraid she would forget where she was and attack me. I also felt deeply sad for her because she was here. *Where was her family? Why weren't they caring for her?* She wasn't going to get the help she needed in here. It was rough not sleeping, but I knew I couldn't afford an incident and I surely couldn't afford to appear "tired." A splash of water on my face was my best friend during those two days.

One instance in particular, I remember eating with the other residents, and this lady kept staring at me. I acted like I did not see her. Again, my goal was to stay under the radar and get out of there as soon as possible. I knew the lady was going for shock therapy because in the middle of the day, they would literally round up the people who needed to go like cattle. It was dehumanizing. I kept eating and she kept staring. I was praying, "Lord, please don't let this lady do something that will cause me to be here longer."

She did not stop staring, and I didn't stop ignoring her. She said, "Hey." I still acted like I did not see or hear her. The lady got a little louder and said, "Hey!" I reluctantly turned in her direction. She stared at me a little more. At this point, I am thinking of just leaving the scene, but there were not many options as to where I could go. She kept staring. Then she calmly said, "You don't belong here." It took every ounce of exhausted strength I had left to not erupt in tears. After she said that, she stopped staring. It was the weirdest thing. It was if God wanted to get that message to me by any means necessary. Although the situation was peculiar, I felt such peace after she said that. I even said to myself while sitting there, "I don't belong here."

God's love reached for me once again. I was in a bad situation, but He affirmed His presence in my life through a complete stranger.

Maybe you feel unlovable and unseen. Let me assure you that God sees you and He cares.

> *Look to the Lord and His*
> *strength; seek His face always.*
> *Psalm 105:4 NIV*

When times of uncertainty creep up on us, we must remind ourselves and each other of His promises. God will certainly strengthen you when you are weak. I am a witness of His love carrying me through the storms of life. He carried me at times that I did not even have the strength to ask Him to do so. He just did it because I am His daughter, and someone else was praying for me. Seeking God's face gets us exactly where we need to be.

> *But You, LORD, are a*

*compassionate and gracious
God, slow to anger, abounding in
love and faithfulness. Psalm
86:15 NIV*

God is so compassionate. He is our Father. Just like a good natural parent, He is concerned about us. He wants to see us grow and mature.

As I discussed in the beginning of this chapter, we all desire true, sincere, love. We want someone to love us for us. But what if the person you believed loved you deeply decided to change their mind? It could be someone you're in a long-term relationship with, or even a spouse. What if they decided to take their love back? What if they stated that they were no longer "in love" with you? What if the person said that they did not even want you anymore? Wow. Hard blows, right? Especially if you have invested years of your life with a person.

I want to encourage you and reassure you that you are enough. You don't have to "put on" for anyone. You don't have to try and earn someone's love. You don't have to sit and wonder if you simply being who God created you to be will fit anyone's agenda. Sis, you do not have to go against your original intent and purpose for acceptance. Most certainly, you don't have to sacrifice your dignity and self-respect for an imitation of real love. If every person who claimed to love you at one point in your life, later decided to change their mind.... God's love for you REMAINS.

Allow His love to take root in you and strengthen you. Let His undying love cover you, yet beautifully uncover your worth. He wants to protect you. You are safe with Him.

Instead of looking to "fall in love" with a man. Live in love. Exist in it. Saturate yourself in God's love for you. It is a love that won't change. It is a love that will never go away. It is a love that will walk with you through any fire you may go through. He will not leave you. He will not give up on you. Love for you kept Jesus on the cross.

And so, we know and rely on the

love God has for us. God is love.

Whoever lives in love lives in

God, and God in them. I John

4:16 NIV

God's love can never be "taken back." It just is. It exists for you and I to dwell in. Our Father will never get up one day and be confused about His commitment and promise to love us. His Word declares that He loves us, and God cannot lie. He does not go back on His Word. His Word is established in heaven.

Your Word, LORD, is eternal; it

stands firm in the heavens.

Psalm 119:89 NIV

God's decision to love you stands firm. He will never stop loving you. Let me say that again, God will never stop loving you. There is nothing that you can do that will change God's mind about you.

And I am convinced that nothing can ever separate us from God's love. Neither death nor life, neither angels nor demons, neither our fears for today nor our worries about tomorrow–not even the powers of hell can separate us from God's love. No power in the sky above or in the earth below–indeed, nothing in all creation will ever be able to separate us from the love of God that is revealed in Christ Jesus our Lord. (Romans 8:38-39)

Once we realize this truth, we will able to exist free of shame.

You may even feel as though your voice does not matter because you're not popular or have "people in high places," that you are able to call on in your life. Let me tell you something, once God's hand is on your life, nothing can stop it. Please don't allow insecurity to stop you from believing that you are loved and that you have purpose. We can beat ourselves up while God is trying to elevate and promote us. He wants to do exceeding, abundantly above all that you can ask or think in your life.

Popularity has nothing to do with the love God extends to us. If you have ever read the story of

David, he was not the popular one. As matter of fact, he wasn't even considered by his father to be a part of the "line-up" when Samuel arrived to anoint the next king of Israel. Saul was the first King (he was rejected by God) and now God sends Samuel unknowingly to anoint David, the little ruddy shepherd boy that no one knew. The obvious, popular choices of his older brothers were rejected too. This story ignites me every time I think about it!

God loved David so much that he was hidden until the appointed time. He was the one overlooked, rejected, and underrated. David's father did not call him to the place that his brothers were invited to with Samuel. David was an after-thought. He was not considered because he was tending to the sheep. A lowly, humbling position. Sis, God loved David so much that they developed a relationship in the pastures. God and David had something going on when no one was around. God was developing David in his unpopular position. It was just God and David. There are times when it is just you and God, and you feel like it is a waste of time because you are hidden. No one sees you. But the very development you're rejecting now because it is "unpopular" will be what you need once you are uncovered. A real revealing takes time and patience.

I am asking you to be patient with the Lord. He is doing something spectacular in you, even in the quiet moments of your life. You're feeling like it's a waste of time. You feel like everyone is being "seen" but you. You're aware of your giftings, and you know God has called you to greater, but it seems like the battery in your watch has stopped. You are on pause. The set place of development is ineffective.

God loves you so much that He will not allow a premature reveal. Trust His timing.

David's progression and road to kingship came in steps, over many years. Once David was anointed by Samuel; he went back into development. He was anointed, and he knew it but God's love for him and His care, kept him hidden until the appointed time.

You are so loved by God that He is taking time to develop you. Your process is not a punishment, it is necessary.

Prayer: God, thank you for my sister. Thank you for her tears, thank you for her hardships. Thank you for the fire that she is in right now. Lord Jesus, please remind her of Your love for her. Remind her of how deeply concerned about her You are. You know the number of hairs that are on her head, that is how into her You are. You make no mistakes, the fire she is in right now will develop her into what You ordained. Father, I ask that Your love begin to blanket her right now. Let Your love and comfort be felt throughout her entire being. God, help us to give thanks to You according to Psalm 136:26 because Your love endures forever. Your love endures through whatever we face, even if our own behavior may have had a hand in where we are currently. Your love still endures, it abides with us forever. God, thank You for first loving us! We are able to love You and others because

You first loved us (I John 4:19). You are so into us that nothing we can do can separate us from the enduring, selfless, deep love You have for us. Thank You for loving us with an everlasting love and drawing us with unfailing kindness (Jeremiah 31:3). Great is Your love for us. I pray that my sister will realize how much she is on Your mind. God, we appreciate You and we trust Your plan even when it does not quite make sense to us. Your love prevails and Your promises are true. Help us to lean on You for Your name is a strong tower (Proverbs 18:10), we are safe with You. Make my sister over in Your love and help her to know that You have it all under Your careful control, in Jesus name, amen.

You Are Healed And Whole

There is a road that you must take to becoming healed and whole. Life can toss us some doozies! It can throw up some real one, two punches straight to the head!

Vaginismus is defined as a condition involving a muscle spasm in the pelvic floor muscles. It can make it painful, difficult, or impossible to have sexual intercourse, to undergo a gynecological exam, and to insert a tampon.

I understand this definition. I lived it for thirty-five years.

Let's go back, so you can understand why I say that there is indeed a road to becoming healed and whole.

I went to get my first pap smear at the age of 24. I was not sexually active but planning to get married the very next year. When people would ask me if I had ever had one, I would play along like I had one before. But I had never had one and I was terrified of it. A fear and anxiety had built itself up in me about it. I also was never able to insert a tampon, ever. Go with me, I'm going somewhere with the story.

While at my pap smear appointment, the doctor could not complete it. I was so terrified. I tried every method I could possibly think of to "relax." I counted backwards, I took deep breaths, I closed my eyes, I listened to music loudly; but absolutely nothing worked. The doctor wasn't aware of Vaginismus which I found to be the running theme throughout the next ten years with every physician I encountered.

He told me to come back once I got married, because after sexual intercourse, I would be able to have the pap smear. That theory proved to be wrong in my case. I went on about my business and I was honest with my fiancé about how the pap appointment did not go well.

Although, it did not go well and I was busy planning a future and a wedding, it bugged me.

It was on my mind. But who was I going to tell that I was going through this? This was 2007, so people were not as "transparent" or willing to openly discuss issues as our society is now. I felt like it was something I needed to hold on to and try to solve myself. The doctor said it would get better, so I held on to that. It will get better. Things got better, but only when I decided to tackle the issue head-on and face all my fears and anxiety.

The year 2008 arrives, and I get married in October of that year. What the doctor and I hoped to happen, did not happen. It did not happen for years, nine to be exact.

Now, I had no idea that I was living with Vaginismus this entire time. I had no idea it developed in me at some point in my life. I was never sexually abused, thank God! So, that was not the issue. But there was no doubt that there was an issue. An anxiety had built up in me unknowingly at some point in my life concerning sexual intercourse, tampon use, and pap smears. Again, I was terrified, but I could not pinpoint when the fear settled in me, it just felt like it had always been there.

A few years passed and in March of 2015, I had a surgery that I believed would cure everything. After visiting another doctor, and another pap smear was unsuccessful. The doctor suggested that I have a hymenectomy. I was totally down for it! If this surgery could improve and cure what I was experiencing, I was completely ready!

I went in for the surgery early in the morning, and the nurse who was assigned to me was such an angel. This was my first time in a hospital for an extended amount of time, let alone having surgery. So, having such a sweet and considerate caretaker helped me tremendously through the process.

Now, I avidly watch Grey's Anatomy, so once they told me that they were giving me

anesthesia to "knock me out" for surgery, I instantly made the decision to try and "stay up" as long as I could. Please don't ask me why I did this, but it was hilarious and fun.

As they wheeled me back and administered that last knockout punch of sedation medication, I remember fighting so hard to stay awake. I remember trying hard to see everything. We entered the operating room and it was so sterile looking, and an ugly color green. On the other hand, that could've been the color I saw because I was high, but who knows!?! Hilarious!

The surgeon told me to count backwards from ten. Honey, I was out like a broken light bulb by "ten." I'm not sure if I even said the whole word, I was gone!

I woke up in recovery, groggy and sore. But I believed things would be better from this point on, so I was tired due to the surgery, yet very hopeful.

Needless to say, I went back to the doctor after healing from the surgery and he tried a pap smear again. Y'all, it failed again. I sat there in disbelief. I was crushed. My confidence was destroyed yet again.

There is something about disappointment that can literally destroy you bit by bit. But only if you allow it. We will discuss that later.

Disappointments in life are inevitable and everyone experiences various levels of disappointment, but there is a way to remain hopeful. As I said, we will discuss this later.

I left the doctor's office stunned. Completely shocked beyond comprehension.

Let me let you in on some of my dialogue with God during these years of turmoil:

God! Why won't You heal me? Why am I going through this? This junk is weird! I haven't even heard of anyone I know going through this! Why did you choose me to go through this!??? This is completely unfair! I waited until I was married to have sex! What am I being punished for? There are so many loose women out here, I saved myself! Why can't any solutions work? What are

You doing? This is dumb!

That was me. I didn't always run down this list of questions and statements, but at moments like having a whole surgery and it did not work.... Oh, I had something to say!

Time then went on.

I had got a promising new job at a major hospital in my town. I mean the place was known for being the best. So, I took advantage of the healthcare and begin to dig into therapy options. A sex-therapist to be exact. I had early morning sessions with her once a week before I started my shift at the hospital.

I was hopeful again. I was taking another step towards being cured of this mysterious condition. Our sessions went well. She made me see and consider things differently, in a healthier way. I started looking forward to seeing her once a week because she was helping me deal with what I was facing head-on. She provided solutions that I desperately needed to hear and know about. She lit up the path I was on with hope again. She reassured me that I was not weird or a broken woman. The situation was present, but I could get through it. I could breathe again.

Our sessions continued and we were getting somewhere. She then encouraged me to try and see a gynecologist again for a pap smear. I did. I made the appointment and I felt empowered. I felt like I could conquer it this time, because of her encouragement.

I called. I set-up the appointment. I went. It was during the workday, so I took an extended lunch, and my therapist promised to be there right by my side, and she was.

This time, they had the idea of using a numbing gel. I was down for the idea. Whatever it took to get it done, shoot.

He proceeded with the procedure. My therapist was holding my hand. Y'all, it did not work, again.

I cried so hard. I panicked. I felt the disappointment overwhelming my entire being once again. Why couldn't I get this right? This simple procedure that women have all the time just was not working for me. That crushing feeling came and sat on me, again.

It was so bad and so emotional, that even the therapist was tearing up. She wanted me to be cured so badly. She had invested time and hope into me. She wanted this for me. I could see the hurt in her eyes too. I felt like a failure.

My ninth wedding anniversary was here. Still no consummation.

In October of 2017, a discussion was had. Maybe our marriage was a mistake. This was too much to endure.

From that month until, January 2018; I searched for answers. Something had to give, seriously. This was unbelievable.

I remembered years ago, surfing YouTube, and seeing a story of a young lady that was unable to consummate her marriage for years. For whatever reason, the memory of the video popped into my mind again, so I looked it up. I watched it. I identified.

There were doctors at the end of the video that made statements about her condition and what she had gone through. They seemed so knowledgeable. It felt like they were talking directly to me. The doctors spoke of their center in New York, and how they were able to help this young lady be cured after years of agony.

I was intrigued. I wanted to know more. Maybe this was finally my answer. The young lady's experience in the video was identical to mine. But I was afraid to try again. Thinking of trying again became too much, it was overwhelming, and it felt like disappointment was inevitable. Disappointment had occurred so many times, I was not sure that this treatment could work. But I didn't have any other choice at this point. I had to try it. I had to try to see past what I thought would happen and see what I was trying desperately to believe that God could do for me. I had to envision my healing. I had to actually see myself in a better position than where I was. That was hard. It was difficult.

I probably watched that YouTube video six thousand times. I watched it morning, noon, and night. I just wanted to convince myself that it would work. I had already been through so much physically, emotionally, and financially trying to find a solution, that I had to gear myself up for this new path I was considering.

One day I was at work, and I left for lunch. As, I sat in the drive-thru line, I watched the video one last time. It was an extremely cold January morning. I will never forget that moment nor my location. It is forever etched in my memory. As the video ended, I felt a prompting to just call them. My heart was sitting outside of my body in the passenger seat of my car by this point. I asked myself, "Am I going to call them?" I did. I Googled their phone number, and I called. I couldn't believe it; the phone was ringing, and I felt sick to my stomach. To my surprise, one of the doctors answered the phone. I choked on my "hello." I was in shock. I didn't know where to begin in the conversation. I was frozen.

"Hello, may I take your order!!" I was so stuck that I didn't even hear the young woman screaming at me through the drive-thru monitor because the doctor answered the phone. I rolled down the window, "I am so sorry miss, can you hold on one second?" I then asked the doctor to give me a second as I ordered my food. Y'all, I was a mess! Why did I call in the drive-thru line before I ordered my food? I told myself to get it together. I then proceeded to order my food. I let the doctor know what was going on, and we talked in between me ordering my food and driving off.

After I drove off, and parked, we really talked. The doctor asked me some questions. I told her about my experiences over the last nine years. She then told me that my story sounded like I indeed had Vaginismus. That statement alone brought a sense of relief. She validated what I suffered silently through for many years. She gave a name to it and identified it. The tears began to flow. I let them.

She told me that she was going to email me all the information that I needed to proceed. The doctor then told me that once I received the email, she wanted me to write my story and send it to them. I am a writer, and I account for events through writing frequently. But you know what I realized. I had never just sat down and wrote about my experiences with Vaginismus. Never. It was locked away. It wasn't something that I had practiced freely discussing. I just didn't talk about it.

The doctor also instructed me to schedule a good time for a Skype session with the two doctors. That part made me nervous. I knew they had seen countless patients suffering with the same thing I was suffering with, but they would see me now. I know. It sounds irrational, but that's where I was. It had taken so much courage to even make the phone call, but now you want to see me. That part made me uneasy. It made me feel like they would judge me.

Again, I know, my thoughts were very irrational,

but you must remember I had already opened myself up to other options that just did not work over a long period of time. Now, you want me to come out of "hiding" and confront this issue, again? What if it doesn't work, again? I would have exposed myself for nothing once again.

On the other hand, it was just something about the YouTube video I watched with them in it. It was just something about the phone call that grabbed me. Once I received the email and begin to review the information, something touched my heart deeply then as well. I connected with the process, even in my nervousness. Then, when I began to recount what I'd experienced over so many years, I felt even more connected. I'd began to tell myself, "This treatment may work."

Well, the Skype session happened. It was a Thursday night in January 2018. We talked. They explained the treatment more in depth and reassured me that I would be cured. I had read on their website that they had "a very high" success rate, so I was hopeful. As we talked, I felt more and more at ease. The only thing that concerned me was the cost of the treatment. It was not cheap. The doctors made me feel like I would be cured. They provided the glimmer of hope needed. Their warm demeanor gave me permission to be hopeful again.

After the call ended, I needed to figure out how to gather the funds for the treatment. There was no way that I was going to let this opportunity pass me. None.

I started to think of all the options. The money was not sitting in the savings account, it just wasn't.

God made a way. Every single dime was provided. God covered every cost. The treatment was taken care of, the two-week hotel stay was covered, and the flights were booked.

The way the funds seamlessly came into place served as a sign to me that God was in it. He made the way plain. He provided every penny I needed for the treatment and traveling costs.

I was beyond grateful.

The date that I picked to begin treatment was March 19th – March 30th, 2018. I flew to New York City on Saturday March 17th. So, from the very first phone call, Skype session and countless emails, I waited almost three months to arrive in the Big Apple. During those three months, I probably watched every YouTube video that the Center posted on their website. There were testimonials from other women who had successfully gone through the treatment program. The words that they spoke filled me with even more hope and faith that I could be cured as well. As I begin to believe more, the doubt slowly begins to disappear. I could feel God reassuring me that I would be ok. Finally.

> *Look to the Lord and His*
> *strength; seek His face always.*
> *Psalm 105:4 NIV*

I was looking to Him for my miracle. My attention was shifting to the only One who could heal me. I had to believe that He could do it.

Everything moved without any hiccups. It was amazing to watch it unfold. I had to ask my job for the time off to go to New York for two weeks. I had to miss two weeks of work.

My manager at the time did not hesitate to approve the time away. She'd known a little about my struggle as a woman who wanted to be a mommy, so she was happy to allow me to go.

One of my sisters encouraged me to vlog while I was in NY. At first, I was like hecky naw, I am not doing that! Then, as I thought about it, I realized that my story could possibly help someone else. I remembered all that time I felt alone and like an alien. I had taken the time to watch so many testimonials of others and it helped me tremendously. Now, it was my turn to give back. I didn't have to keep this issue a secret anymore, I was being prepared to be healed. I ended up vlogging each day that I was there, and it was the best decision I could have ever made. I will forever have the memories documented of when I was healed, and someone who is currently experiencing Vaginismus would be able to gain hope and faith through my experiences. It was a win-win!

The weekend I arrived, there was a nor'easter. Now, I am from the Midwest, so I know about snow. But y'all, this snow was weird. It was a lot and it just dumped out of nowhere. I'd brought my tripod for my vlog, so I took my tripod outside and took pictures, in the snow. It was great! It was freeing! It was warm. There was plenty of snow around, but it was warm. Again, weird.

I vlogged before my very first session on Monday, March 19th, 2018. I was excited and nervous. I stayed at a hotel that the doctors suggested, and I am so glad that I did. The room was decent, (I am a bit of a hotel-snob) and the hotel served free breakfast and dinner every weeknight. The waffles were my favorite and the topping choices made my heart happy every morning that I was there because breakfast was served daily. With the hotel serving free yummy meals, that helped me save a ton of money when it came to food. I was so grateful.

When I arrived for my first session, I emerged out of the uber vehicle almost on the verge of real crocodile tears. I was here. I was at the therapy center. I was at the place that I watched countless videos about on the internet. It was surreal. It was overwhelming, but in a good way. I forgot to mention that the doctors left a gift for me at the front desk and they encouraged texting and calling as I traveled. I felt extremely supported and never alone through the process.

Once I entered the building, I was warmly greeted and told the doctors would be out to see me momentarily. I sat down and I begin to look through the large, oversized book filled with testimonials of patients who had come to the therapy center and were cured. An overwhelming feeling of joy and hope swept over me. I was finally here. I was where I would be healed and cured. My testimonial would be placed in this book after it was all said and done. I knew it and I believed it.

When one of the doctors came out to greet me, it felt familiar. It felt right. I knew her and she knew me. Plus, we had the Skype session and stayed in close contact from that point to the very moment I arrived at the center. She was so welcoming! It put me even more at ease. As I was beginning my journey, another young woman who was at the end of hers came out of the back of the office as well. She looked so happy. She looked refreshed. She looked relieved.

The doctor had to tend to something else in the back and she asked if it was ok if the young woman shared some of her story with me while I waited for her return. I agreed. The young lady and myself went into what I would later learn was the "chill room." We sat down, and she begin to share about what brought her to the center and her journey since she'd been there.

The young woman was from all the way across the world. She was from a completely different continent. The beautiful thing about the center is that they literally help women from around the world. The center has been in existence since 1996, so you can only imagine the countless number of women that had attended before I arrived in March of 2018.

As she shared, I listened. I soaked up everything she was saying. She was so sincere, and there was a glow of freedom all around her. She'd suffered silently for years just as I had. There was an instant connection between us. We still talk to each other and check on one another to this day. I am thankful for that!

Our conversation was almost like a passing of a mantle. She encouraged me and let me know that I could do what needed to be done to be cured. She reassured me that I would be cured. I think almost every young woman that experiences Vaginismus, with failed attempts to be cured, secretly doubts if they will be cured or not; upon arriving at the center. I believe it's just human nature to doubt the process, especially after so much consecutive disappointment. I felt so empowered after speaking with her. I sensed that she was a quiet person, but there was an undeniable boldness that exuded from her now as a healed woman.

Over the next two weeks, I would discover a completely new level of strength within myself. I was stretched mentally and physically. I was stretched beyond what I thought I was capable of.

Before I left for treatment and the months leading up to my arrival, I trained my mind to believe. Yes, I retrained my mind to only believe that I would be healed. Of course, I still struggled with doubt at times, but my main focus was believing that the treatment would work for me and that I would be healed.

There were various things that I applied in treatment and it worked. I moved through treatment very quickly. I believe I progressed so quickly because I was tired of suffering, the cost of treatment was not cheap, God was with me, and I was determined to experience healing. I most certainly experienced the most freeing and liberating two weeks of my life.

At the completion of treatment, the doctors stated that I was one of their best patients. I couldn't believe it. I asked them if they were serious, and if that was something that they told everyone. I was in shock and honored because I'd realized just how many countless women they'd helped over the years. For them to state that I was one of the best touched me deeply. I was grateful that God was with me. He helped me through every step of the process. I remember the very first physical session I had, I cried so hard and the doctors had to wait to proceed and they calmed me down. So, to go from that extremely anxious young woman, to where I was at the completion of the treatment was magnificent.

On one of my last days there, the doctor and I were coming from the back, and there sat a new young lady beginning her journey that day. The doctor told me she had to go to the back to finish up something and asked if I would go to the "chill room" and encourage her. Aha! It clicked. The one cured encouraged the new unsure one coming into the center for the first time. I gladly obliged.

The young lady and I headed into the room once she agreed, and I began to share glimpses of my story. I saw hope being infused into her. I saw strength rising in her. I saw my words empowering her to believe that she could be cured too. It was beautiful. It was refreshing. It was everything.

I later released my vlogs on YouTube. It took some guts to do it, but I knew I had absolutely nothing to be ashamed of. A big portion of my purpose is encouraging others, so I had to be who God created me to be and release the vlogs. Discussing any issue in life is difficult, but discussing sexual issues is especially difficult. I wish that such issues were discussed more openly in the Christian setting among women. We are sexual creatures.

Life is created and enters the earth through sexual intimacy. Sex is natural. It is beautiful when it involves two consenting adults. Once I released my vlogs, my inboxes on various social media platforms blew up with messages. There are women out there suffering silently all over the globe. My videos gave them a voice. I was thankful that I didn't allow fear to keep me from sharing. I did not go through Vaginismus just for my own growth and development in life, but I went through it to help the next young woman believe again.

One of the assignments once you leave the center is to book an appointment for a pap smear. Even after all the trauma I'd experienced with past pap smears, there was no fear. I was excited to conquer one more thing on this healing journey. I made that appointment immediately, with no hesitation.

I ended up having an appointment in May of 2018. I took a pregnancy test at the doctor's office, and it came back negative. I was a little disappointed, but I was ok with it because we were actively trying, and God knew when I would conceive. I needed to trust that process as well.

I wholeheartedly believe I was pregnant then, but it was too early to be picked up by the over the counter pregnancy test. One week later, I took another test and it showed double lines everywhere! I was pregnant! I took several tests just to be sure! Several!

Vaginismus is a portion of my life story. I accept that now. I understand process. I understand that many things that occur in life are completely out of our control. All we can do is decide to trust God through it all.

Sis, I ask that you don't beat yourself up because of your process. Go through it, but don't let it tear you down. If you allow the process to work for you, you will choose to be thankful through the ups and the downs. It will be exceedingly difficult at times, but you can do it. Learn the lesson, whatever the lesson may be for your life. Maybe it's not Vaginismus, but you're experiencing something you don't understand and you're waiting on God to heal you.

Don't allow the negative words of others taint your belief that God is able to do anything.

You Are Not Damaged Goods

*Now to Him Who is able to do far
more abundantly beyond all that
we ask or think, according to the
power that works within us.*
Ephesians 3:20 ESV

I was out to dinner with a friend and I was experiencing some difficult hardships, it was obvious. We were eating dinner and I was trying to play it cool. You know how we do when we are hurting; we hide. I was trying so hard to hide.

But, if a person really cares about you and is in tune with the Holy Spirit, it doesn't matter if you sat there in shades and a smile, the person would see you clearly. She saw me clearly. I felt like what I had experienced in life and what I was currently experiencing, disqualified me from being loved. I felt damaged. I felt tossed to the side. I felt empty. She looked at me and said, "You are not damaged goods." Y'all, I cried so hard in that upscale restaurant. I am positive that I was judged by one or two people sitting there. I mean, I was crying big, ugly tears. The kind of tears that make your face do weird things, and it gets worse if you try to make it stop. Those were the kind of tears I was crying. But I could not help it, I could not hold it back any longer. She saw me. She saw the pain, and she saw the uneasiness I was walking with. The enemy is such a liar. The dude is the father of lies. He will do everything he can to try to plant seeds of doubt in your mind about God and yourself.

I am not damaged goods. Sis, you are not damaged goods. It does not matter what you have been through, trials don't disqualify you. Trials qualify you to compassionately help someone else. The enemy wants you to shrink back in embarrassment. God wants you to rise in His strength. Once you are made whole, there will not be one thing that a person can do or say to cause you to believe that God does not love you deeply, intentionally, and beyond comprehension.

Your process may be similar but never completely identical to someone else's. As you experience the process, please do not "beat yourself up." The process comes to refine and renew. As believers, we must understand that the fire does not come to harm us, but it comes to benefit us. You may be in a situation for an exceedingly long time. People may not understand it. You may not understand it. Often, when people don't understand something, they may try to present solutions that really don't help. They may even place blame on you for something that is just as much out of your control as it is theirs. Please never allow harsh opinions to destroy what God is doing in you. He is not doing it in "them." He is doing it in you! I will not deny the fact that words hurt, and words can be very impactful. But the only words that can define you are contained in the Bible. His words about you are what matter, and those words should hold the heaviest weight in your life.

During those nine years, I wish that I had allowed the Word to take root in me more than I did. I grew up in church, so I am familiar with scripture. I have studied scripture throughout the years, so I know scripture. But, allowing the Word of God to take root in you is something totally different. Think of the roots of a tree. Once it is planted and begins to grow and stretch out below the ground, it is extremely hard to dig up the root. The tree is established. The tree is strong. Even when a storm comes and knocks down a tree, you ever notice how the stump is usually still there? The top of the tree can be destroyed easily, but those roots will remain. Roots stay planted in the storm. When you allow His Word to take root, that is when you truly become healed and whole.

One of the most important keys to experiencing healing and wholeness in your life is keeping the right surroundings. That just doesn't include people, but it includes everything you consume. Everything that you allow in your space should foster healing and wholeness. Be careful of what you say. Be cautious of what you watch and what you listen to.

You must speak it, believe it, and declare; "I am healed, and I am whole."

Heaven wants to intervene, give permission by using the power of your words.

> *You will also declare a thing,*
> *and it will be established for*
> *you. So, light will shine on your*
> *ways. Job 22:28 NKJV*

Prayer: God, thank You for my sister that is believing You for healing. Thank You that by Your stripes we are healed. Thank You that we can come boldly to Your throne of grace (Hebrews 4:16). God, we have access through the cross and by the power of Your blood. Any issues that we face never take You by surprise

God. You know everything about us, You even know the number of hairs on our head. You are all-knowing and all-seeing. There is nothing that we can keep from You or hide from You. Even if we decide to make our bed in hell, Your eyes are there too. God, my sister needs healing and she needs to be made whole. Just like the woman with the issue of blood, we know that if we can simply and intentionally touch the hem of Your garment, we can and will be made whole. God You desire that we be whole. We desire truth in the inward parts God. Our help is in the name of the Lord, the Maker of heaven and earth (Psalm 124:8). We have hope in You God. We have peace in You

Savior. We know that everything we experience is only working together for our good. Lord, please send the answers and solutions that my sister needs. God, we know that You hear even the faintest cry. You hear us when we pray, and You are concerned about us. I pray that my sister learns how to cast her cares on You (I Peter 5:7). We don't have to be anxious or carry our pain and uncertainty. You took care of that at Calvary. Thank you, God, for being our strong tower, we can run to You and be safe (Proverbs 18:10). I pray that my sister is filled with joy even in the process of becoming who You made her to be (John 16:24). God You came so that we could have life and have it to the full (John 10:10). Anything that she may be facing now that is robbing her of joy and a full life, God I pray that You would begin to open her eyes and her heart to You. It is in You that we have everything we need. It is in You that we can and will be healed and become whole, in Jesus name, amen.

You Are Safe, Rest

Being aware that you are safe can and will cause peace to flow in your life. When you feel unsafe in your environment, or in your relationships, there is an unrest that occurs.

At the end of 2019, through the very beginning of 2020, I felt like the Holy Spirit was instructing me to "rest." But it was not the kind of rest that demanded sleep or slumber, it was the kind of rest that called for peace of mind. I needed to rest in my mind and rest in my emotions. I needed to know I was safe, and that rest was possible.

As women, often we can become so caught up in life, and in serving others that we forget that we ourselves need TLC as well. It is a common theme among women to forget to "rest." Psalm twenty-three is the scripture that reminds us that we are safe, and we can rest because God has us!

The Lord is my Shepard (to feed, to guide and to shield me), I shall not want. He lets me lie down in green pastures; He leads me beside the still and quiet waters. He refreshes and restores my soul (life); He leads me in the paths of righteousness for His name's sake. Even though I walk through the (sunless) valley of the shadow of death, I fear no evil, for You are with me; Your rod (to protect) and Your staff (to guide), they comfort and console me. You prepare a table before me in the presence of my enemies. You have anointed and refreshed my head with oil. My cup overflows. Surely goodness and mercy and unfailing love shall follow me all the days of my life, And I shall dwell forever (throughout all my days) in the house and in the presence of the Lord.

What a promise! God says that even in your valley experiences, I will provide rest. He will also provide refreshing, and goodness and mercy will follow you. Picture that for a moment.

God says that even in your most trying moments of life when everything looks and feels out of whack, goodness and mercy will still follow you! Whew! That is absolutely amazing. Sis, even when you feel like your world is unraveling at a rapid speed, you will still have the favor of God with you!

God is so dope! His promises are true, and He is incapable of lying to us!

Have you ever been experiencing a really challenging situation and it wasn't the easiest thing to take time to rest? With God, He will set you up in His "heavenly spa" even in those times of uncertainty. He will allow you to lie down in green pastures (picture it) and lead you beside still and quiet waters.

One of my favorite things to do is to take walks by the ocean. I love everything about taking in a sunrise on the beach and listening to the sound of the ocean. It relaxes every part of my mind, and body. What amazes me even more is that although all that water is present, God has it set up that it is contained. The water will softly wash up to the shoreline of the beach, then flow right back to its appropriate position. I am safe and I can rest during those beautiful early mornings. Can you imagine God taking your hand and leading you beside the still and quiet waters?

The amazing thing about walking with God and allowing Him to lead is that He won't ever lead us down the wrong path. It certainly takes trust and faith to follow Him though, because some of those paths look scary and uncertain. Think about it for a moment. God led Jesus down a path that did not appear promising at all. First, He was born to a virgin girl who had zero "status." Mary was not famous, she did not have a lot of money, and she was not the "prime" candidate for birthing the Savior of the world. Then, once the birth was getting ready to take place, she was on the run to make sure that Jesus wasn't killed. On top of that, they could not find anywhere "comfortable" to have the birth of Jesus. Y'all, they had to settle for a barn, a stable. Jesus was laid in a manger in "rags." A manger is a structure used to feed animals. The King of heaven and earth was laid in something used to feed animals. His debut was nothing but lowly. But He was safe. The conditions were not ideal in the least bit, the scene wasn't comparable to something that you've always imagined. In today's world, Jesus and His family would've been laughed at. The dialogue would go something like this: "So, you're telling me that the King of kings and Lord of lords, the Prince of peace, the Messiah; He was born in a stable?"

The status of His arrival did not match the status of who He was. As women, I believe that's what becomes challenging for many of us. We want the status of who God promised we are to match every-single-last-one of our life events. That narrative is false, and it messes with our minds as well as our faith. If Jesus had to endure unfavorable circumstances; sis what makes you believe that you will not have to endure the same?

Even after the birth story of our Savior, His life was low-key. He did what He needed to do and spoke up when needed but Jesus was about His Father's business. He was not interested in doing anything out of time or out of season to impress not one person. He desired to move in the timing of God. He was following His lead daily. The ultimate purpose of Jesus being born, and living was to shed His blood and die for the sins of the world, then be buried and rise again in three days. Does that not sound scary and uncertain? But it was all for purpose and Jesus knew that. He stood on it. Even in the garden when He prayed and said, "If it be Your will, let this cup pass," He submitted to the will of His Father. He knew He was safe trusting God and following His lead.

Our paths may resemble heartache instead of triumph for the sake of purpose.

I am learning that lesson. I am grateful for the lesson. If God holds my hand and leads me, I can rest. I will be alright. There will be times I cry, times it hurts tremendously, and times I will be confused as to how God will get glory out of it, but bottom line, I am safe.

Jesus fulfilled His purpose and endured the pain of the cross. But, without His sacrifice and obedience, we would all be lost. Are you bucking against a hard process? If you don't understand what God is doing with your life, do you let go of His hand? I encourage you to hold on to Him even tighter through things that just don't make sense. Yield to His will for your life and what He wants. I am a witness that He can use the "hard stuff" for His glory. Safety, rest, and peace in Him often looks turbulent at first. It is true, God uses pain to reveal His glory.

His word encourages us to cast our cares/anxiety on Him because He cares for us.

> *"Give all your worries and cares*
> *to God, for He cares about you." I*
> *Peter 5:7 NLT*

God is fully aware that we will experience things that may make us feel anxious or worried. You will experience these feelings, especially if your life is submitted to Him. Human logic and understanding are always at war with the Spirit of God. There are battles in our minds and in our bodies that we war with daily! There is no escaping it, but God has provided outlets. He invites us to not carry what we battle with; He asks us to cast it all on Him. It may seem like a good idea at the time because you're desperately trying to figure it all out, but it is a horrible idea to stay up all night worrying. Worry is a road to nowhere. Well, I take that back. Worry is a road to more worry and unrest. Who wants to live like that? The best thing we can do is take advantage of the beautiful offer God has provided us with. He wants to carry all that worry for us, so we can fully trust Him and His plan for our lives.

Choosing to live in peace is a conscious decision that must be made every single day. God provides peace but we must choose to exist in it. Now, this is something I am still mastering. But the more life experiences I have, and the more I see God literally pull me out of "hard things," I am leaning on Him more and more. His track record is flawless. I will trust the One Who never fails.

Sometimes, it just takes us "taking a beat." Like literally stopping and evaluating our emotions and our responses.

Will this response be beneficial in the future?

Will my response bring peace or more tension?

Will my response reflect that of a Kingdom citizen?

I know! Initially, it is difficult to think like this in the heat of things because emotions are running high and most people want to be sure that they come back strong. But what if you said nothing at first and then took your time to respond. It will be challenging, but you're more likely not to say something you may regret later. It is always worth taking the beat for the sake of peace in that moment and in the future.

During the month of December 2019, I had an experience and encounter with the Holy Spirit that I will never, ever forget. One of my sisters and I were meeting at my spiritual mom's home almost every Monday evening. It was essential to my sanity. I was already experiencing some difficult circumstances for a few months by the end of the year, that seemed to be only getting worse. I remember it just being an extremely tough time for me. Imagine someone trying to walk a long distance through deep mud in the middle of a thunderstorm; that's what every day for me felt like. It was just plain old rough.

So, because of my history and past experiences with difficulty; I determined within myself to lean into God HARD. I mean I was determined to not go under at all. I was letting God handle it. I was actively casting my cares, worries and anxiety on Him. It was a purposeful and conscious decision. I was not going to let depression win my mind ever again. I was purposely gathering with friends almost every Monday evening to pray and seek God's face. It was one of the most empowering decisions I have ever made. I am a firm believer in reaching out for help when I need it. I suffered silently for too many years in my life when all I had to do was ask for help. God places loving people in our lives to help us when we need it. I didn't need money or material possessions, I needed friends that would earnestly pray with me. I am so grateful God provided just that!

One Monday evening in December, we gathered, and the Holy Spirit came too. I first received the Holy Spirit when I was thirteen years old. This night resembled that night, but it was so different all at the same time. I remember just asking God to help me, because I felt my mind not comprehending what was occurring in my life and it hurt me deeply. That is how depression starts. The person just wants the pain to stop, and they can't figure out how, so they just succumb to the pain. I was determined not to do that. I wanted to find my rest and safety in Him. I knew it was available and I wanted to really experience it in my life. I wanted to take my little hands off it, and really trust God.

"Trust in the Lord with all your heart and lean not on your own understanding; in all your ways submit to Him, and He will make your paths straight." Proverbs 3:5-6 NIV

I wasn't looking to place blame or figure it all out anymore. I wanted rest.

As we prayed, I remember laying there on the floor and tears were streaming down my face. I couldn't say anything lofty, I just cried and worshipped God. That was all I had. As I was laying there, a song began to play and it was, "Safe In His Arms," by Vickie Winans. That song is very old, but at that moment, it was the sentiment of my heart. I just wanted to feel safe.

While the song played, I felt a release that I hadn't ever felt before. I felt the comfort of the Holy Spirit. He was with me. He was there. He heard me. The lyrics to the song still speak to me even to this day.

"Because the Lord is my Shepard, I have

everything I need. He lets me rest in the meadows grass and He leads me besides the quiet stream. He restores my failing hands and helps me to do what honors Him the most. That's why I'm safe, safe in His arms. When the storm of life is raging and the billows roll, so glad He shall hide me, safe in His arms."

I felt every lyric of that song. God walked me through every verse and showed me just how safe I was with Him, even in the middle of a confusing storm.

While the evening progressed, it felt like minutes, but it had been hours of just being in the presence of God. He sent refreshing. He covered me in His peace, His safety, His rest and His love. I felt like I could literally leap over mountains and run through troops. God strengthened me beyond my own strength and comprehension. I could make it now. Just to give you a glimpse of how amazing and awesome the experience with God was, my friend had to drive me home because I was so engulfed in the presence of God. He is so kind that He allowed me to experience His presence in that manner. God knew what the road was up ahead, and He knew I would need His strength and power to stand. I am so grateful.

I was reading a scripture and simultaneously having a discussion with a friend about it, and something jumped out at me that I had never really considered before.

> *"Then you will experience God's peace, which exceeds anything we can understand. His peace will guard your hearts and minds as you live in Christ Jesus." Philippians 4:7 NLT*

Once you ask God to help you and decide to exist in Him, His peace will take care of your heart and mind. Most times when individuals are hurt in relationships of any kind, it causes that person to put up barriers and walls. There was a song that said, "I got this ice box where my heart use to be." Many of us take on this mentality. We will protect ourselves by any means necessary. So much so, that the barrier of "protection" we've thrown up in defense of the "bad stuff" has also blocked any of the "good stuff" from penetrating as well. God can turn any heart of stone to a heart of flesh, but we must submit it to Him. God is not forceful; He is a gentleman. He offers, He speaks, He confirms; but He will never force anything on you. He gave us all free-will. You must choose Him. You must choose His way.

Sis, you will not have to put up barriers. God has promised that His peace will guard you. Take a moment and visualize a secret service agent. They are generally always "on guard." So much so that the dignitary they are protecting can perform their duties as needed without worrying about guarding themselves. They are aware of the protection around them, so they don't concern themselves with being restricted in how they live. The secret service takes care of all of that for them. I believe that's how God protects us.

Of course, we need to use wisdom when it comes to our hearts and minds, because they are vital to our peace, safety, and rest. God promises to keep the person in perfect peace who keeps their mind on Him.

> *"You will keep in perfect peace*
> *all who trust in You, all whose*
> *thoughts are fixed on You."*
> Isaiah 26:3 NLT

Sis, you don't have to worry about creating that ice box around your heart. God wants you whole. He wants you to trust in Him. He wants you to trust that He has your heart. You can rest and live at the same time. Rest in Jesus. He had a plan for your life before you were even thought of! Who better to trust than the One Who knows absolutely everything about you? Your heart is safe in Christ, live.

There is a story in the bible about a woman caught in the act of adultery. (John 8) Jesus was teaching to a crowd, and then the teachers of religious law and the Pharisees brought a woman before Him who had been caught in the act. They placed her in front of the crowd, they did not interrupt politely; it was very abrupt. They wanted to embarrass her.

The law stated that she was to be stoned, so they asked Jesus what should be done to her? The Pharisees were basically trying to trip Jesus up and trap Him into saying something that could be used against Him.

I absolutely love the response that Jesus gave; it was epic! He simply stooped down to the ground and wrote in the dust with His finger. Who does that? Epic!

The Pharisees kept demanding an answer even though Jesus was not providing one, He was writing in the dust. Jesus finally answered and stood up and said, "Let the one who has never sinned throw the first stone!" Sis, then Jesus stooped down again to write in the dust!!!! Epic moves!

When the accusers realized what Jesus said,

and they realized that they had absolutely no case; they backed away one by one. You know how when you were a kid and you asked your parent for something and they hit you with the, "But did you clean your room yet?" You stand there realizing what they said, you let it sink in, then you realize you are not worthy of what you're asking your parent(s) at the moment because you have not fulfilled something they requested of you, first.

The accusers slipped away from the scene, and Jesus was left in the middle of the crowd with the woman. So, Jesus stood up again and asked, "Where are your accusers, did not even one of them condemn you?"

The woman answered, "No, Lord." Jesus responded, "Neither do I, go and sin no more."

I can only imagine how she felt during the entire ordeal. The men were out to embarrass her and to kill her. But the interesting thing is that they were just really using her and her situation to "get Jesus." They really were not concerned for this woman's well-being.

114 | P a g e

Their plan did not work. It failed miserably actually.

How many times have people tried to trip you up? Or maybe they have accused you of something that you actually did, but did it in a way to embarrass you or humiliate you?

The bible says that Satan is an accuser of the brethren. He accuses us before God day and night. The beautiful truth about Jesus is that He did not condemn the world, He came to save us.

That woman was still before a crowd. The woman was still embarrassed, I am sure of it; but she was left with Jesus. She was now safe and forgiven.

There have been times in my own life where people have brought up the worst things about me in an effort to tear me down and destroy my self-esteem. At first, it worked, but then I remembered Who I belonged to.

Sis, no matter who tries to bring you down,

accuse you, tear you apart, or even embarrass you; you are safe with Jesus. Lean in on His word and what He declares about you. Drown out the noise of the accusers and walk in the liberty that the Holy Spirit provides.

The only One qualified to throw the stone, didn't.

Prayer: Father, thank You for my sister. Thank You that Your love and compassion are covering her even in this moment! God, I ask that You allow her to feel safe. Safe in Your arms. Safe in Your Will. Safe in You and the plan You indeed have for her life and for her future. You don't leave us desolate and alone when we go through life. You protect us and our hearts with Your compassion and undying love. Every wall of defense that my sister has placed up in her life and around her heart, I pray in the name of Jesus that she will realize that You alone are her covering and her protection. She does not have to allow the root of bitterness or malice to be present in her life. Help her to find the strength to rest and live in You! You provide rest and strength! God, Your joy is our strength!! Help her to read the twenty-third Psalm and take it to heart. Every single word is Your promise to her! God You love us, and You desire for us to be whole! God, I ask that You renew and restore my sister. Speak to her now, at whatever phase of her life she is in! Give her joy unspeakable and full of Your glory! Her flaws, past issues, present struggles, and failures are all covered under Your blood! Help her to realize this and walk in the freedom and joy Your Spirit provides! The only One qualified to throw stones is You, and You have never thrown stones at us; You have only extended grace, love, compassion, forgiveness, and favor. God, I thank You that she is safe with You and she can rest in your love. In Jesus name, amen.

Here are a few scriptures to lean on in times that you struggle to feel safe in Him:

- Proverbs 18:10
- Psalm 91
- Psalm 16:11

- I Thessalonians 3:16
- Matthew 11:28

You Are His

I believe that as believers, we experience certain situations solely designed to bring God glory. Lately, I have really been pondering on the scripture that calls for us to be salt and light in the earth.

> *"You are the salt of the earth......You are the light of the world." Matthew 5:13-16 NLT*

The taste of salt is very evident, you cannot mistake it. Actually, pouring too much salt can ruin a meal and ultimately make it taste disgusting. There is a balance and a harmony that must be present between salt and the food it covers. There cannot be too much and there can't be too little.

Light is essential to our lives. It is extremely hard to exist without light, especially at night.

It is difficult to "hide" light. The presence of light causes darkness to give way and disappear.

God asks us as His children to be salt and light in the world. Our presence gives light to everyone we encounter. The people impacted by the light we carry must see God in us. The hope is that they will see Him in what we do and how we conduct ourselves and glorify our Father that is in heaven.

Experiencing hardship should cause the light in us to shine even brighter. Although sometimes hardship can cause us to back up from God, as His children, we should desire to draw even closer. I have found that even if we are unaware of the "shine" in us, God will send people to confirm that it is indeed there. At this moment, my life is in the middle of something difficult, but so many people whether I know them or whether they are complete strangers have stated that there is a "glow" about me. That for me confirms that God can use you even in the middle of our trials. He can use us even more in heart ache because our hearts are more open and sincere towards Him in the fire.

When we go through hard things, sometimes it is difficult to even see how God will get the glory out of it because it just seems altogether unfair. You almost ask yourself as you're experiencing the hardship, "Why am I going through this again?"

It is in those really tough times that you discover just how much God is into you and loves you. He loves you so much that He desires spiritual development and maturity to be present in your life. The only way to reach such maturity is hardship. The only way an olive can become olive oil, is through crushing. That's just how it is sis!

In the middle of it, it sucks. It sucks really bad. Sometimes, you just want out! In your mind you're like, "I did not sign up for this." Oh, but you did! The moment you surrendered your life and said yes to being His, is the moment your development began. God uses every circumstance in our life to perfect us and cause us to glow in the world even more. Let the process be what it is sis, don't take back your "yes."

Going through things usually pushes us towards God. We pray more, we are more in tune with what He's saying and how He desires to move in our lives. Trials usually cause a more open dialogue between us and God. We want to know Him, and we want to know what's up. We want to know how all of this will work together for our good. God invites us to call unto Him.

> *"Ask me and I will tell you*
> *remarkable secrets you do not*
> *know about things to come."*
> *Jeremiah 33:3 NLT*

That is absolutely remarkable to me! God is literally inviting you and I to know secrets, and to know about things to come. God will reveal and He does lead and guide, but He rarely if ever gives us the entire picture. I believe this is so, because as His children, He desires that we seek Him often and sincerely. He desires a relationship with us.

Our human relationships can encounter so much throughout our lives, some things that are great and some things that are not so great! Sometimes in romantic relationships, we give our all and some more! But, what if one day the man you love deeply states that he is no longer "in love" with you? What do you do? How do you react? Can this statement cause you to think less of yourself? Absolutely! Especially if you've invested a lot of time into the relationship, and somehow lost sight of your importance to the Kingdom of God.

Human feelings change and fluctuate. A person can be passionately loving towards you one day and the next day completely flip the script. A lot of times, the flipped script really has nothing to do with you, but everything to do with the state of that individual.

Our hearts are fragile and loving another individual romantically can certainly tap into those more fragile parts of our hearts. We must remain rooted and grounded in the love of our Savior even while being in a relationship with a man. That balance gets thrown off sometimes. Sis, get back in balance. Jesus loves you deeply for eternity.

Now, whether a man says he loves you or not, you have to be secure in the truth that God loves you deeply and intentionally. That love will never change. You are His.

Back in my elementary, middle school and high school days; I was heavily involved in sports. I believe that involvement kept me from trouble and certain experiences in my life. My dad drilled into my head that my responsibility was to get good grades and be a great teammate on the court. Those two things were my focus from early on. My father traveled with me all over the state to play basketball for years, even while he was working two or three jobs to make sure our family was supported well. I can remember him being at everything I did. One memory that sticks out in particular was a daddy-daughter dance we attended. I can remember my mom getting me dressed and doing my hair to go to the dance with my dad. I was so excited! My dad took care of me that day, I felt like I was on a date. It was just he and I and the other attendees. I felt special. I felt like a princess. I felt protected. I knew my daddy was going to protect me, I wasn't worried about anything but having fun.

That's how our heavenly Father cares for us and takes care of us. He desires that we live life to the full! He shields us, He protects us, He keeps us, He is present with us. I spent a lot of time with my dad growing up, most of my memories include him being right there with me. An earthly father-daughter relationship mirrors the relationship our heavenly Father desires to have with us.

Being God's daughter is the best thing there is! As His daughter, you have access to what is His. You have access to His peace, love, joy, strength, and your inheritance. A good father will never withhold something that His daughter needs. He may make her wait on certain wants because He realizes she is not ready or mature enough to handle it, but his desire is to provide what his daughter needs. Every single last one of us has a certain process that we must go through, and it's different for each person. If you are one who desires God's perfect will to be done in your life, there are some things that you will have to endure. God's plan includes pain sis. Yes, pain. God uses pain because it produces power, strength, and it uncovers the intention of your heart. Think about it, the bible says that God so loved the world that He gave His only begotten Son. God allowed His only Son to come to earth and serve with the mission to die for the sins of the world. The plan included death. His perfect will included pain. But there were also triumphant moments, and moments to celebrate.

Maturity is birthed through painful moments in life if your focus is on taking up your own cross and following Him.

"Then Jesus said to His

disciples; If any of you wants to be my follower, you must give up your own way, take up your cross, and follow me." Matthew 16:24 NLT

As His daughter, a decision must be made to take up all your pain, hard experiences, difficulties and still follow Jesus wholeheartedly. In the middle of things that hurt, God still desires that we choose to follow Him. The most beautiful thing about it is that you may be hurting deeply and don't quite understand your current circumstances, but God promises to give us beauty for ashes. He will not allow His daughter to suffer only, there is good that will come out of it, if you just hang on!

Sis, you will never experience anything in life that God has not already seen. He is aware of every single thing occurring around you and in you. He knows you as His daughter! Honestly, that is what provides comfort for me. God knows.... everything! Absolutely nothing takes Him by surprise. He knows the end from the beginning.

> *"Declaring the end from the beginning, and from ancient times things that are not yet done, saying; My counsel shall stand, and I will do all My pleasure." Isaiah 46:10 KJV*

He just knows, and He sees, and He cares. I wouldn't want to trust a God who knows as much as I do, or just a little more than I do. I cannot trust that type of leadership. Your Father knows it all, and He wants to lead and guide you into all truth. To have true relationship with Jesus, there needs to be such a dependence and a trust in Him and His word. He will never ever fail you as your Father. He will never leave you as your Father. He will always support you as a Father. He will always care for you as His daughter. He will always have your best interest in His heart for your life. You can completely trust His timing, His ways, and His promises.

If you had a good earthly father or not so good earthly father, that doesn't qualify you nor disqualify you for the love of your Heavenly Father. He desires a relationship with you, His daughter.

Prayer: Father, thank You for my sister who is praying for better days. Thank you for my sister who is experiencing better days and wants to make sure that You remain the head of her life and decisions. Thank You God for how You cover us as Your daughters! God, my prayer for my sister is that You would continue to reveal Yourself to her more and more. As she draws near to You, I pray that You draw near to her. Let there be a relationship and sweet communion. Thank You for loving us as Your own. You died so that we could live! God, she is not only Your daughter, but You call her a friend. No greater love is this than a man who would lay down His life for His friends. Thank You for calling her

friend! Friends share things with one another. Friends tell each other about themselves, and they are open about their love and devotion to one another. It is a privilege to be called friend by the King of kings and the Lord of lords! We honor You today Father, and we thank You that You are our Daddy, Abba, Father! Help my sister to realize her true identity as Yours for eternity. You love her assuredly and deeply! Help us to know it and walk in it!! In the precious name of Jesus, amen.

In The Thick Of Hard Things

Remaining hopeful in disappointing times in your life is plain difficult. Although it is difficult, God has given us many tools to remain hopeful.

The book of Job is a perfect example of someone in the thick of hard stuff yet remaining hopeful. His own wife told him to go ahead and curse God and die. Satan hand-picked Job and presented his case before God, and God allowed the circumstances to occur. The enemy told God that if He removed the hedge of protection around Job and his household, that Job would surely curse God to His face. Although God allowed it, He told Satan, you can touch everything Job has in his power, but on Job himself (his life), do not touch him.

"The Lord said to Satan, Very well, then, everything he has in

your power, but on the man
himself do not lay a finger." Job
1:12 NIV

Job was hit hard! One messenger would be coming to inform him of horrible things happening around him, and another messenger would be right behind that one to report tragedy as well.

Can you imagine receiving one bad report after another, with no breaks?

Job indeed came to what we would call a breaking point, but his response was still to worship God.

"At this, Job got up and tore his
robe and shaved his head. Then
he fell to the ground in worship
and said: Naked I came from my
mother's womb, and naked will I
depart. The Lord gave and the
Lord has taken away; may the
name of the Lord be praised. In
all of this, Job did not sin by

charging God with wrongdoing."

Job 1:20-22 NIV

That stance is absolutely remarkable! It is admirable! Job was devoted to God even in the face of losing everything, including his own children.

In chapter two, Satan is relentless. He accuses Job some more, for absolutely no reason. God allowed his family and possessions to be destroyed, and now Satan wants permission to strike his body.

"The Lord said to Satan, Very well, then, he is in your hands, but you must spare his life." Job 2:6 NIV

Job was then afflicted with painful sores from the soles of his feet to the very top of his head. Pause. Take a moment and think about how you would feel in this situation. This is some very thick stuff! You have already lost everything of importance to you, and now your body is attacked! Where do you go from here? What

should be your response? Do you give up at this
point?

Job's own wife could not even understand his
commitment to withstand what they were
experiencing, she told him to curse God and
just die.

> *"His wife said to him, Are you*
> *still maintaining your integrity?*
> *Curse God and die! He replied,*
> *you are talking foolish woman.*
> *Shall we accept good from God,*
> *and not trouble?" Job 2:9-10 NIV*

Whew! What faith!! By this time in scripture,
Job had not received the Holy Spirit because
Jesus hadn't come on the scene yet. Y'all, Job
was devoted without the indwelling of the Holy
Ghost. He had such respect and honor for God,
without even receiving the promise of the Holy
Spirit. He just believed and had deep faith. That
is remarkable to me!

Now, Job's human side did show up, but he still
didn't curse God, he did curse the day he was

born.

> *Turmoil causes us to reflect and think. Job did that. His hope in God was solid though. Job stated that even though God was allowing him to be slain, his hope remained in Him. Job 13:15 NIV*

Job did not quite know what was at the end of his affliction, or if it would ever end. He didn't know, only God knew. But he trusted Him. That trust, faith and hope made the difference. The situation looked and felt embarrassing and shameful, I am sure of it. When we experience hard things that just don't make sense or make us look like we are in sin, it hurts. We must go through it, there is no escaping it, and that is often the most difficult part. You mean to tell me; *I have to go through this publicly? You mean everyone will know? You mean this could ruin everything I ever built? You mean to tell me that friends and family may have another opportunity to look at me cross-eyed? They will have the chance to speak on my situation without knowing what the end will be.*

As I have stated already, God already knows the end from the beginning, but when you're in the thick of hard things, it can be difficult to keep that perspective. I am speaking from experience!

I was having a conversation with my mom in the winter of 2019, and I was expressing to her that I felt as if I had to go through some peculiar things in my life. Some tough stuff! Some stuff most people would not survive, and surely would not still desire to serve God through. From Vaginismus, to depression, to suicide attempts, to marriage troubles, to losing my very first baby; I mean just tough stuff! It makes me wonder and ask God questions. Overall, though, I know He has a plan. He had a plan before I experienced any of those things! Pain produces power, it's just God's way! It hurts in the process, but there is a beautiful end to the pain and suffering. God promised that if we suffer with Him, we will reign with Him.

> *"If we suffer, we shall also reign*
> *with Him; if we deny Him, He*
> *will also deny us." II Timothy*
> *2:12 KJV*

My close friends often speak of my resiliency to me, but there is no doubt that if God was not present with me every single second of the day, I would not be here. Facts.

I appreciate the love, but I know I am nothing without the love and safety found in Jesus.

Going back to what I stated about Job, he went through all that calamity in his life, and he wasn't even a blood washed believer! Sis, you, and I have the Spirit of the Living God dwelling on the inside of us! We can go through some hard stuff and still come out victorious! There is no doubt! The same power that raised Jesus from the dead, abides in us! There is absolutely nothing that you cannot overcome with the help of the Holy Spirit! Will it be hard? Absolutely! But God says that you are more than a conqueror!

> *"No, despite all these things,*
> *overwhelming victory is ours*
> *through Christ, Who loved us."*
> *Romans 8:37 NLT*

Overwhelming victory is yours Sis! Victory will take over! It will overtake you! It will envelop your entire being! The key to this level of living is allowing the Holy Ghost to do what it was sent to do! Sis, you must step aside and allow the Spirit of God to comfort you, send peace and guide you through it all!

Job's situation looked hopeless and like it would never be turned around for his good. It looked and felt bleak as ever! Have you ever been there? I know I have. Bleak situations are perfect set-ups for God to be God. He can take the impossible and create the possible.

> *"After Job had prayed for his*
> *friends, the Lord restored his*
> *fortunes and gave him twice as*

much as he had before." Job
42:10 NIV

Yes, you read that correctly. After Job prayed for others even in the midst of his own pain, the Lord restored his fortunes, and even gave him back double. I believe that once we learn to serve others and sincerely pray for others, even when we are going through horrible things; God will see our sacrifice and bless us. Please don't pray for others just to be blessed! God wants us to do it from our heart. If we do it from our heart and from a pure place, I believe He will see us and send just what we need. Being a Christian is about love and service. If you don't possess this in your walk, you are missing the point of it all.

Job's story proves that God can and will restore! You must endure those seasons that seem like they will never end or work together for your good. For example, how will losing my first baby work together for my good? I have no idea at this moment, but my trust and faith must lie with

God through whatever I go through. It is my responsibility to love, serve and pray for others, even in my painful experiences. Then, when I acknowledge my pain but still desire to serve, I am becoming more like Christ.

Faith must be at the center of your trials. It must be! God's word says that it is impossible to even please God without it.

> *"And it is impossible to please God without faith. Anyone who wants to come to Him must believe that God exists and that He rewards those who sincerely seek Him." Hebrews 11:6 NLT*

Why would God want us to trust Him and have faith even in the thick of hard things? I believe He wants to show us His power and just how much He loves us. He desires to receive the glory and honor through every situation you face. He wants glory out of your life and your existence. What better way to honor God than with your life?

God, thank You for my sister today. Jesus thank You that you see her and that You love her. Thank You that You have promised to never leave us nor forsake us. You have promised to be a very present help even in the time of our troubles. God, my sister is in the thick of hard situations in her life. I pray that You would comfort her and surround her mind with Your peace. Help her to keep her mind on You. You promised to keep her mind in perfect peace if she keeps it stayed on You. It is so easy for our minds to drift and for unbelief to creep into our hearts and minds. Some things just seem unfair, but we know that You are a just God. Nothing gets past You, You see it all and You are aware. Thank You for keeping us through things that make no logical sense. Thank You that You have a plan for my sister's life! It is a sure plan! It is a plan that was established before she was even born or thought of! Thank You for the peace and love that You will cover her with today and every day in Jesus name, amen.

You Are Favor

As a woman, you are a carrier of the favor of God. The bible even speaks of the favor that you carry.

> *"The man who finds a wife finds*
> *a treasure, and he receives favor*
> *from the Lord." Proverbs 18:22*
> *NLT*

Sis, you must be that treasure and embody the favor of God even before he finds you.

Favor must be a part of who you are, for it to be woven into the life of your husband, and those in your life.

Experiencing difficulties in your life does not disqualify you from being God's favor, it qualifies you even more. Being tried in fire causes you to come forth as pure gold. Trials build character and cause you to learn how to totally depend upon God for everything. Fire refines us.

"These trials will show that your faith is genuine. It is being tested as fire tests and purifies gold---- though your faith is far more precious than mere gold. So, when your faith remains strong through many trials, it will bring you much praise and glory and honor on the day when Jesus Christ is revealed to the whole world." (I Peter 1:7 NLT)

A woman who honors God carries the favor of God wherever she is, no matter her current relationship status. It doesn't matter if you're single, dating, engaged, married, separated, divorced, or widowed; if you have decided to honor God with your life; you are His favor.

There was certainly a time that I would've said

that this scripture only applies to a wife. On the other hand, I have experienced different relationship statuses in my life as a woman, but none of the titles have caused me to lose the favor of God in my life. One day, I was in the shower and I was crying because I've known for years that I was supposed to write a book. I was crying and asking God to help me think of new ideas. The book title and idea I'd carried and begun working on; no longer "fit" my life at the time. The book was about marriage. I was stuck. Then, God reminded me of one of the chapters that I'd written for the first book. The chapter was called, "You Are Favor." God begin to comfort me even in that moment of despair and mourning of my dream. He reassured me that I still carried the favor of God, even through this very difficult storm in my life. I am His daughter, and a woman of God first. I must believe that God has me no matter what I experience. I must believe that the most important relationship is the one between He and I. In honoring that relationship first, I embody His favor. I embody His grace and His love.

I was having a conversation with a friend about being His favor, and we begin to talk about how differently some young women would view themselves if someone was telling them that they carried the favor of God even from a child. I believe some women today would view themselves differently. I believe they would carry themselves with more dignity and respect. I believe they would not allow just anyone or any man to speak into their life. The woman would be cautious and understand the favor of God present in her life.

How can a wife bring favor into her husband's life without first carrying the favor of God in her own life?

Asking God for wisdom helps us as women of God to grasp who we really are. Wisdom opens our understanding and allows us to live the life that God intended for us to live. Wisdom helps us to avoid traps and things in life that will bring harm to us. Sis, sometimes wisdom may have you standing alone in some seasons, because you value the instructions and voice of God over the voices of people. Don't be afraid to seek wisdom and use it in your life. God even tells us to ask for it, He gives it generously.

> *"If any of you lacks wisdom, you should ask God, who gives generously to all without finding fault, and it will be given to you."*
> *James 1:5 NIV*

Sis, while you are moving through life, you want Godly wisdom leading and guiding you. It's the best way to live your life, because even in experiencing times that you can't quite understand; the One leading you knows it all.

As a woman of God, one who truly strives to live for Him, you carry His favor. You are representation in the earth of the favor of God. Whoever finds you and makes you their wife will gain favor as well, just because they are in covenant with you. But, before that happens, make sure that you carry His favor now, in every single day of your life. You are walking, talking, breathing, existing, tangible favor!

Sis be favor in the way you behave. Be favor in the way you speak and declare. Be favor in your mannerisms and how you carry yourself. Be favor in your thoughts. Pray and ask God to show you how to represent His favor in the earth.

With what you have experienced so far in life, you may be one of the ones who say that you can't possibly be His favor, but that's the furthest thing from the truth. Allow every hard experience to draw you closer to Him. Ask God how would He like to use what you have been through for His glory.

You may be in the middle of heartbreak and disappointment, but even in that experience, you remain to be His favor. Represent!

Prayer: God, please allow my sister to see the

beauty in being Your favor. Allow her to see how You have chosen her to help someone else with what she's been through. Help her to see and realize that it wasn't just for her. Everything we go through and experience; good or bad can and will help someone else! As a woman of God, help her to see that she cannot be selfish in her walk with You. You have called us to help and uplift one another. In our pain, You can produce glory! Help her to be a carrier of Your favor even in the middle of pain. I pray that the light of Who You are will shine brightly in her and through her. Thank You God that we know that we are Your favor in the earth and it is our responsibility to live and walk accordingly. Thank You for being so patient, so good, and so kind to us, in Jesus name, amen.

About The Author

Andrea Renee' is a graduate of Eastern Michigan University with a Bachelor of Science degree in Communication. Her minor during undergrad was Journalism. Andrea is a passionate speaker and writer.

Her goal is to actively encourage and uplift others through the Word of God and her own life experiences. Andrea believes that nothing is wasted, and everything that we go through is meant to assist us in growing and helping those around us.

Andrea desires to inspire women and let them know that anything is possible through Christ. Purpose and love drives Andrea.

Andrea loves to travel, has an online fashion boutique, a blog, and a YouTube channel.

Contact:

authorandrearenee@gmail.com

www.authorandrearenee.com

Please consider leaving an honest Amazon review upon completion.

15382494R00086